— Book *of* —

Quotes *and* Sayings

2

UNIVERSITY
COLLEGE FALMOUTH

— BOOK of —

ILLUSTRATED

QUOTES *and* SAYINGS

Paper supplied by Howard Smith Papers

Printed and bound by R Booth Ltd, Mabe, Penryn, Cornwall

Design by Peter Bennett, St Ives

Production Stuart Odgers

ISBN 978-0-9505680-3-4

Louise Egger

UNIVERSITY
COLLEGE FALMOUTH

— BOOK *of* —

ILLUSTRATED

QUOTES *and* SAYINGS

COMPILED BY THE
BA (HONS) ILLUSTRATION
STUDENTS

University College
FALMOUTH

BA (hons) Illustration

Steve Jackson

This volume is the second book in our series 'Illustrated Quotes and Sayings' and celebrates the work of our graduating students, 2007. It is also the first to be afforded its launch at the Royal Society of Arts, London.

Like our previous editions, this volume will become an important illustration source book for publishing, advertising and media professionals, providing the industry with a rich vein of creative talent to draw from.

As you will see, there is an abundant array of styles and visual languages with standards of innovation, professionalism, and approaches remaining as high as ever, showing that our students represent everything that is best in creative practice.

Heather Rothwell

Hannah Cumming

Alan Male
Programme Leader
BA (Hons) Illustration

Paul Conway

This new body of work by Falmouth graduates shows the distinctive qualities long associated with the College. Drawing remains central and is apparent in the initial selection of students and encouraged and sustained for the duration of the course. The work is recognisably 'Falmouth' but there is no 'house-style' as such. Quite the opposite in fact. The 'Visual Language' of Falmouth is one of great variety and innovation and an obvious enjoyment in the making of the work. What makes it really special, however, is the determined professionalism and an awareness of who the work is for.'

Enjoy.

Thomas Egan

Lisa Zibamanzar-Mofrad

Michael Foreman 2007

Michael Foreman 2007

ROBERT ALLWOOD

'They always talk
who never think.'

Matthew Prior

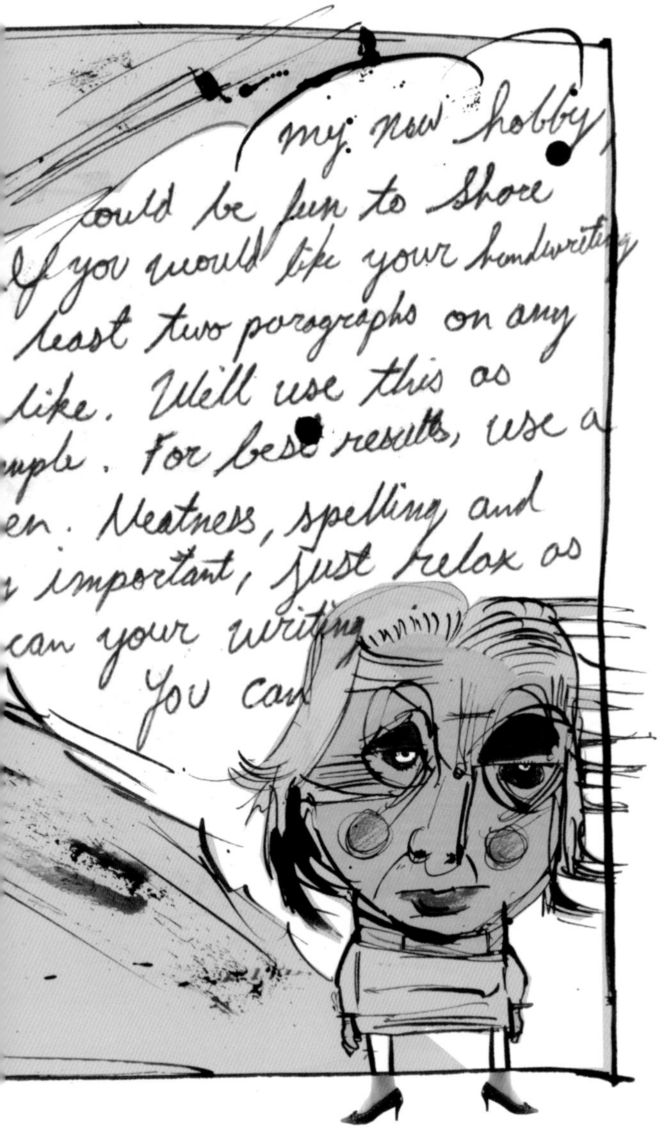
my new hobby
ould be fun to Shore
f you would like your handwriting
least two porographs on any
like. Will use this as
mple. For best results, use a
en. Neatness, spelling and
important, just relax as
can your writing
You can

SCARLETT ALLIER GUTTERIDGE

'The way to read
a fairy tale is to
throw yourself
in.'

W.H. Auden

SOPHIE BANKS

' "Yes," said the farmer. "There are more birds about than usual.'

The Birds
Daphne du Maurier

'Caterpillars do
all the work,
butterflies get all
the publicity.'

George Carlin

'It is difficult to produce a television documentary that is both incisive and probing, when every twelve minutes one is interrupted by dancing rabbits singing about toilet paper.'

Rod Serling

'You arrive
every day to
a different place,
and
sometimes
something you
don't expect at
all becomes a
magical
moment.'

Keren Ann

ROBIN BOYDEN

'I'm not afraid of dying, I just don't want to be there when it happens.'

Spike Milligan

ZOE BRYANT

'Great minds think alike.'

Anon

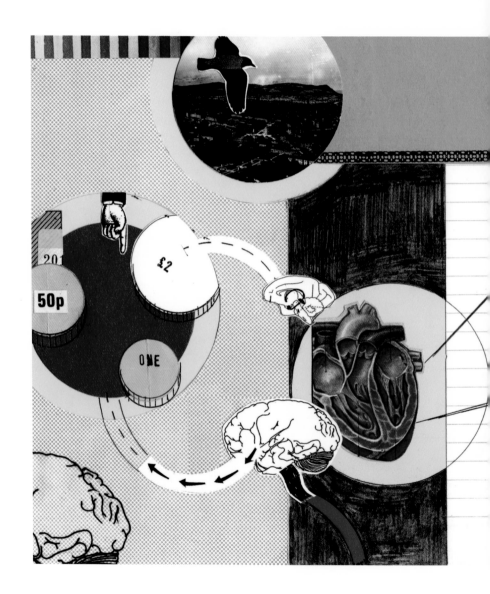

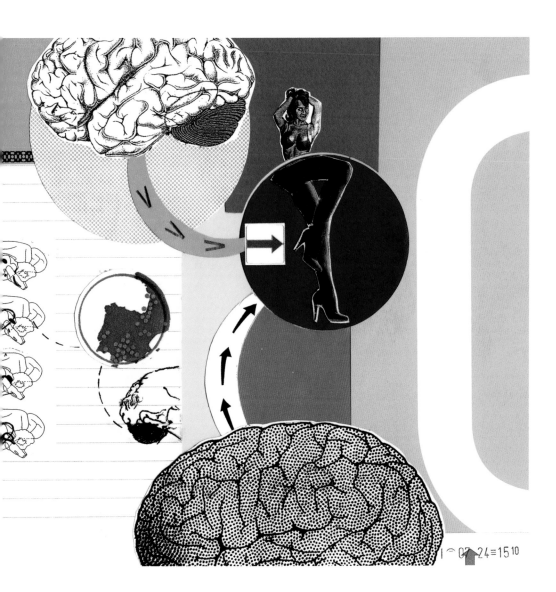

GENNA BYRNE

'Life itself is the
most wonderful
fairytale.'

Hans Christian Andersen

'Shame on you,
Mr. Bush, shame
on you. Any time
you got the Pope
and the Dixie
Chicks against
you, your time is
up.'

Michael Moore

PAUL CONWAY

'All that glitters
is not gold.'

William Shakespeare

IAN COPE

'Every child is interested in nature. You've only got to look at a four-year-old turning over a stone to know that. If you lose that connection, you've lost something precious.'

Sir David Attenborough

JAMES COTTELL

'If God intended
for humans to fly
he would have
given them
wings.'

Anon

ELEANOR COX

'Metaphysics is
a dark ocean
without shores or
lighthouse,
strewn with
many a
philosophic
wreck.'

Immanuel Kant

34

SARAH CROKER

'Atishoo!
Atishoo! We all
fall down.'

Nursery Rhyme

'In an
interstellar burst
I am back to save
the universe.'
Radiohead, Airbag

'A book is good
company.'

Henry Ward Beecher

HANNAH CUMMING

PATRICIA DEERY

'On one issue at
least, men and
women agree,
they both
distrust women.'

Henry Louis Mencken

KASIA DUDZIUK

'One must ask children and birds how cherries and strawberries taste.'

German playwright/poet

THOMAS EGAN

'Every time a
child says, 'I
don't believe in
fairies,' there
is a fairy
somewhere that
falls down dead.'

*James M. Barrie,
Peter Pan*

'America is a vast
conspiracy to
make you happy.'

John Updike

'Autumn
wind of eve,
blow away the
clouds that mass
over the moon's
pure light
and the mists
that cloud our
mind, do thou
sweep away as
well. Now we
disappear, well,
what must we
think of it? From
the sky we came.
Now we may go
back again.
That's at least
one point of view.'

Hôjô Ujimasa
1538-1590

'I think animal
testing is a
terrible idea…
they get all
nervous and
give the
wrong
answers.'

Peter Kay

'I never saw any good that came of telling the truth.'

John Dryden

LISA FORD

'Dancing is like
dreaming with
your feet.'

Orson Welles

JASMINE FOSTER

'She forgot where
she was and fell
among the
poppies, fast
asleep.'

L. Frank Baum
The Wizard Of Oz

'A square peg in
a round hole.'

English Idiom

KJERSTI KAROLINE FRETLAND

FIONA GOWEN

'Sights seen in
the mind's eye
can never be
destroyed.'

Philo of Byzantium

'I can do anything!'

Rose Hacker aged 100,
Journalist
for the
Camden
New Journal.

RACHEL GREEN

page vi.

64

BJORN HOLTER

'Don't disturb my circles.'

Aristotle
Last words before he
was killed by a Roman
soldier while drawing
on a dust board

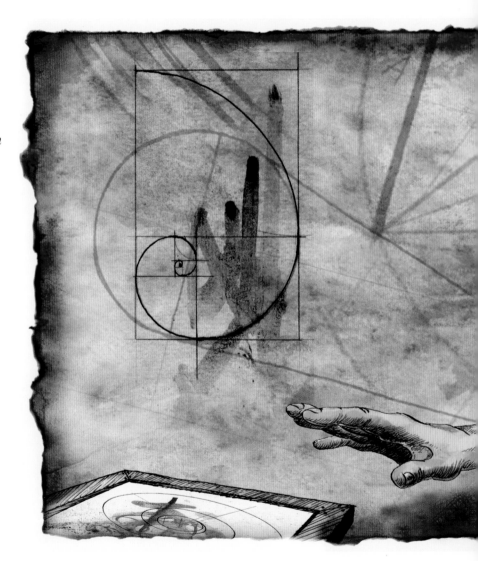

'They (our army) are but the scum of the earth … it is quite amazing what fine fellows we can make of them.'

Arthur Wellesley, Duke of Wellington 1769-1852

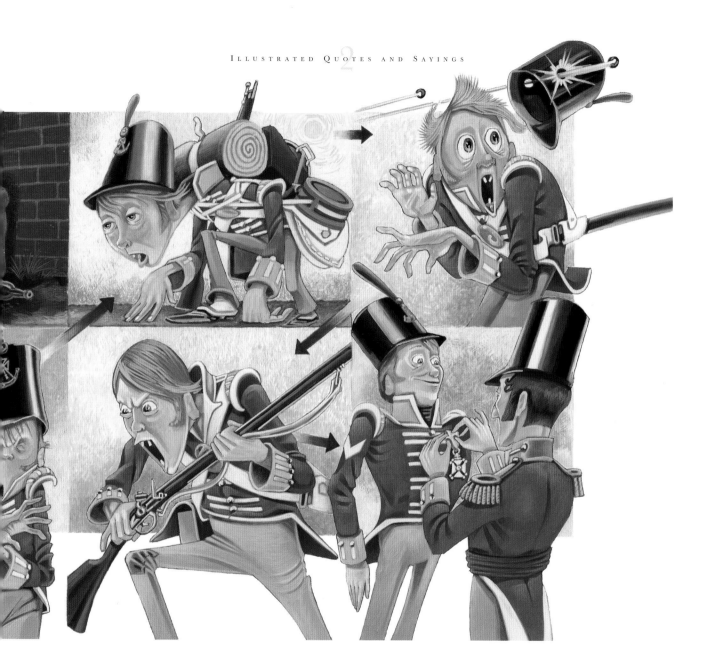

'FRENCH red is best for the HEART'

- New Scientist

JANE LAURIE

'God loved the
birds and
invented trees.
Man loved the
birds and
invented cages.'

Jacques Deval

the REaSonABle maN ADapTs HimSelf To tHe WORLd-
The UnReasONabLe MaN ADapTs tHE WorlD to HImsELF...

-GEOrge BErnARd ShAW

'Flowers grow
out of dark
moments.'

Cortia Kent

CHLOE LUXFORD

'I was one of the
'puzzle children'
myself - a
dyslexic ... you
have a challenge,
never quit!'

Nelson Rockefeller

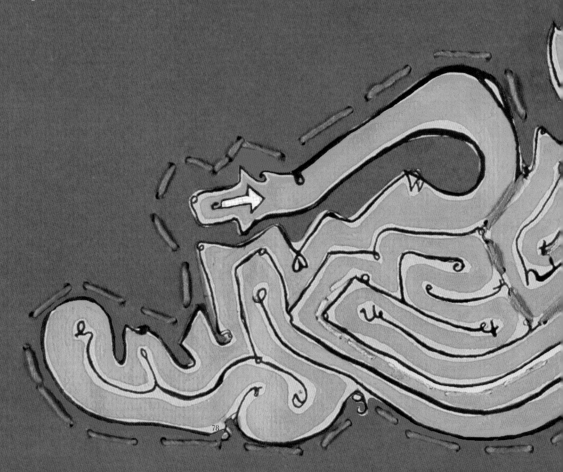

78

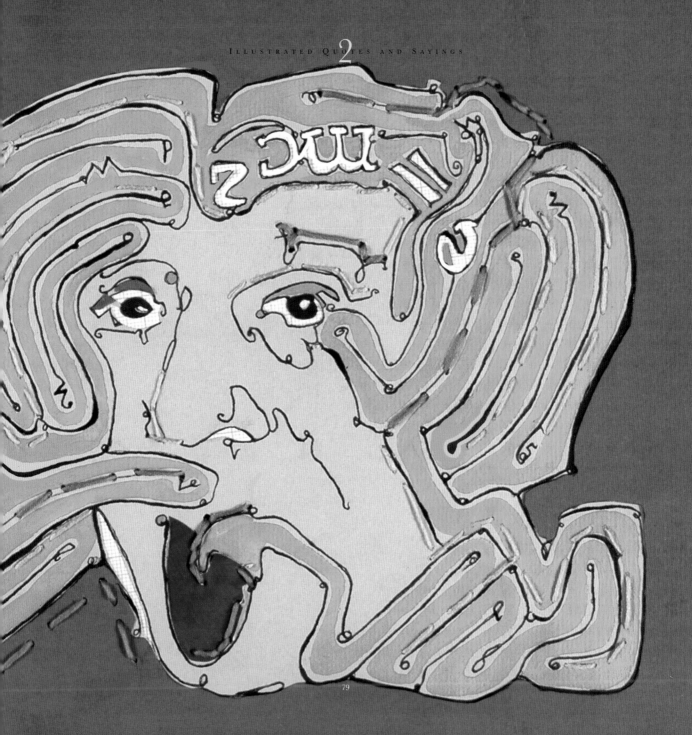

JENNY MARSHALL

'Tell me, O
Octopus I begs,
is those things
arms, or is they
legs? I marvel at
thee, Octopus;
If I were thou, I'd
call me Us.'

Ogden Nash

SHUN MATSUZAKA

'Nature arranges
it so that we
can't shut our
ears but that we
can shut our
mouths.'

Anonymous

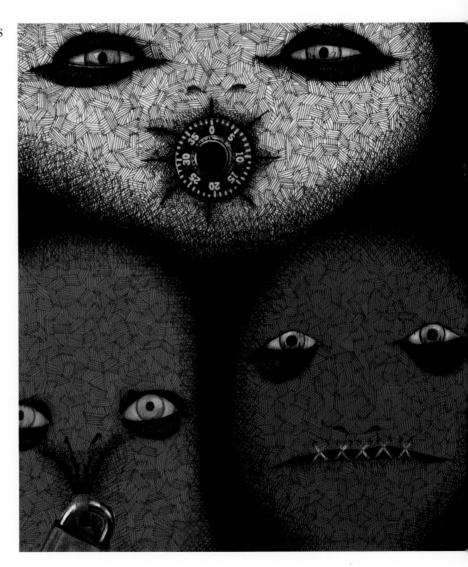

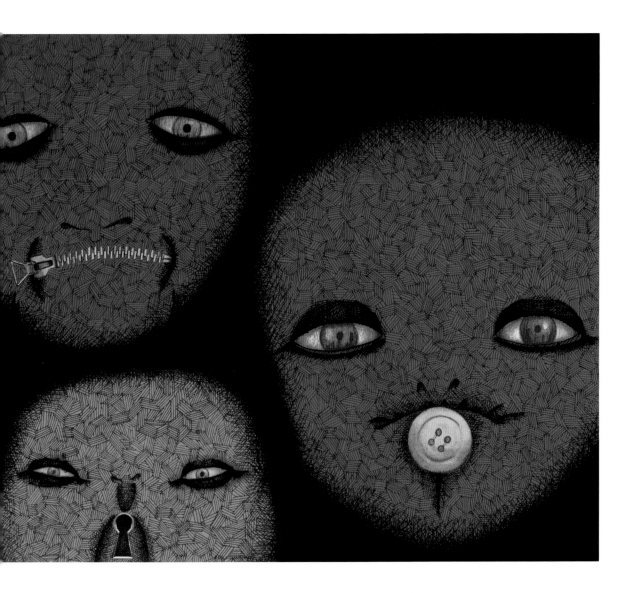

'One in ten fish
are scared of
water.'

Andy Riley

'My music is best
understood by
children and
animals.'

Igor Stravinsky

BENJAMIN MOUNSEY

'It ain't easy
being green.'

Kermit the Frog

LAUREN NICKLESS

'The imaginary
world has always
been the most
fun place for me
to be.'

Claire Forlani

LEWIS OLD

'Did my heart love till now; forswear its sight, for I never saw true beauty till this night.'

William Shakespeare

92

R . I

'Medusa had
locks of serpents
and a gaze that
transfixed the
beholder, turning
him to stone.'

Ancient Greek Myth

DAVID PLANT

'You can't just let
nature run wild.'

Wally Hickel,
former Governor
of Alaska

2

'...utterly romantic, this lonely building on the cusp of land and sea, sending out light into the darkness.'

Jeanette Winterson

'Budgies can
count up to
three.'

*Scott, Budgie
Enthusiast*

'There is nothing
either good
or bad but
thinking
makes it so.'

*William
Shakespeare*

'Eating a
rainbow of foods
is seriously good
for our health.'

Sarah Jones

ELLIE KATE SANDFORD

'Television has
proved that
people will look
at anything,
rather than each
other.'

Ann Landers

KINE SOLBERG

108

'Let's Dance.'

David Bowie

FATIME SZASZI

'Thou know'st
'tis common;
all that lives
must die,
passing through
nature to
eternity.'

William Shakespeare

AMY TIMMS

'Love Me, Love
My Dog.'

English Proverb

TAYNEE TINSLEY

'I am not interested in money, I just want to be wonderful.'

Marilyn Monroe

' "Help me. Save me from hanging!" said the soldier. Those dogs took the judges and all the council, some by the leg and some by the nose, and tossed them so high that they came down broken to bits.'

The Tinder Box
Hans Christian Andersen

CARYS WILLIAMS

'The belly rules the mind.'

Spanish Proverb

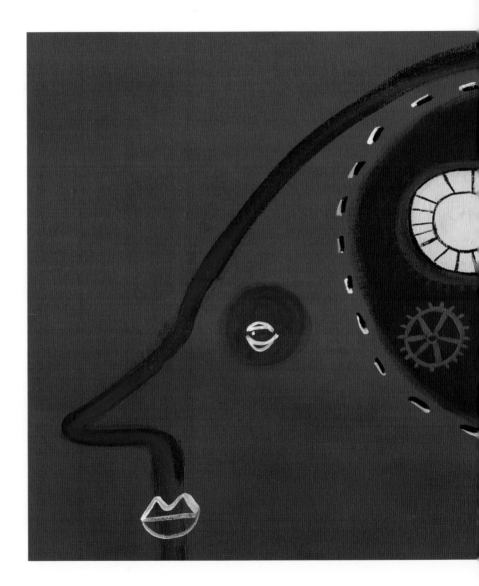

'Let some of the
tranquility of the
cat curl into me.'

*David Harold
Rowbotham,
The Creature in the
Chair*

Fridge Pickers wear Bigger Knickers

'Let them eat cake.'

Marie-Antoinette

LISA ZIBAMANZAR-MOFRAD

124

UNIVERSITY
COLLEGE FALMOUTH
— BOOK *of* —
ILLUSTRATED
CONTACTS

8

Robert Allwood

M: 07854043734
E: robertallwood87@hotmail.com
W: robertallwood.co.uk (under construction)
Myspace page:
7myspace.com/noiseballoonsofthemind

16

John Bennett

E: soveryspecial@hotmail.com
W: www.johnillustration.co.uk

A

10

Scarlett Allier Gutteridge
94 Killigrew Street
Falmouth
Cornwall
TR11 3PT

M: 07885581140
E: runawaykitty@hotmail.co.uk
W: runawaykitty.co.uk

18

Rachel Boulton
21 Paternoster Close
Waltham Abbey
Essex
EN9 3JU

M: 07941844276
E: rmboulton@hotmail.com
W: scribbledot.com

12

Sophie Banks
126 Oxford Gardens
London
W10 6LY

M: 07940660914
E: banksysoph@hotmail.com
W: sophiebanksillustration.co.uk

20

Robin Boyden

M: 07736936590
E: robcore@msn.com
W: robinboydenillustration.com

B

14

Louise Bartlett
Glebelands
Boraston
Tenbury Wells
Worcestershire, WR15 8LH

M: 07980307749
E: LouiseBartlett85@hotmail.com
W: www.Louiseillustration.co.uk

22

Zoë Bryant
Dever Lodge
Micheldever Station
Winchester
Hants, SO21 3AL

M: 07708514524
E: zoeebryant@aol.com
W: zoebryantillustration.co.uk

Genna Byrne

M: 07813253911
E: gennabyrne@hotmail.co.uk
W: gennabyrne.com

James Cottell
Laurel Cottage
Isle Abbotts
Taunton, Somerset
TA3 6RH

T: +44 (0)1460 281550
M: 07729864702
E: Jamescottell70@hotmail.com
W: jamescottell.co.uk

Joe Chin-Quee
29 Old Hill Flats
Falmouth
Cornwall
TR11 2PR

M: 07773009528
E: joechin-quee@hotmail.co.uk
W: joechin-quee.com

Eleanor Cox

T: +44 (0)7817 626604
E: giraffethepellyandme@yahoo.co.uk
W: eleanordown.co.uk

Paul Conway
9 le Fernery
Vallee Des Vaux
St Helier
Jersey

T: +44 (0)1534 887016
E: pc030600@yahoo.co.uk
W: paulconway.co.uk

Sarah Croker
155 City Road
Tilehurst
Reading
Berkshire
RG31 4SL

M: 07806252955
E: sarahillustration@hotmail.co.uk
W: sarahillustration.com

Ian Cope
21 Gyllyngvase Terrace
Falmouth
Cornwall, TR11 4DL

M: 07800517682
E: copeillustration@hotmail.co.uk
W: iancopeillustration.com

Ellie Cryer
Westlea
Blackgate Lane
Henfield, West Sussex
BN5 9HA

T: +44 (0)1273 492442
M: 07734866158
E: tattoosoftears@hotmail.co.uk
W: www.tattoosoftears.co.uk

Hannah Cumming
21 Pengarth Rise
Falmouth
Cornwall
TR11 2RR

M: 07725512813
E: Hannilu@aol.com
W: hannahillustration.com

Louise Egger
4 Spring Rise
Wells
Somerset
BA5 1UE

M: 07870495947
E: loulahoop@hotmail.com
W: http://www.louiseegger.com/

Patricia Deery
32 Culmore Road
Derry
N. Ireland
BT48 7RS

M: 07743069910
E: trishadeery@hotmail.co.uk
W: trishadeery.com

Lloyd Ellison

M: 07727056106
E: Lloyd.Ellison@googlemail.com
W: lloydellison.co.uk

Kasia Dudziuk
38 Georgeham Close
Wigston
Leicester

E: KasiaDudziuk@aol.com
W: www.kasiacreations.co.uk

Clare Elsom
8 High Street
Wheatley, Oxford
OX33 1XX

T: +44 (0)1865 872716
M: 07730652816
E: clare_elsom@hotmail.com
W: elsomillustration.co.uk

Thomas Egan
3 Dalton Street
Douglas
Isle of Man
IM1 3JT

T: +44 (0)1624 672223

Vanelle Fong
Flat 16
G/F, Block C, Shun Chi Court
Kwun Tong, Hong Kong

T: +44 (0)7766551904 UK
    (852)62829127 Hong Kong
E: vanellefly@gmail.com
W: vanellefly.co.uk

Lisa Ford

M: 07919311332
E: lisafordillustrator@hotmail.co.uk
W: lisafordillustrator.com

Rachel Green
7 Sharp Road
Bury St Edmunds
Suffolk
IP33 2NB

M: 07716931970
E: rgreen72@hotmail.com
W: greencrayon.co.uk

Jasmine Foster
3 Greenbank Cottages
Crossroads
Chacewater
Truro, Cornwall
TR4 8QG

M: 07710977329
E: Jazzy328@hotmail.com
W: Jasminesumbrella.com

Bjørn O. Holter

T: (+47) 98622961 Norway
E: email@b-holter.com
W: b-holter.com

Kjersti Karoline Fretland
Engene 84
3012 Drammen
Norway

M: 07875248285
E: kjersti_karoline@yahoo.com
W: kjerstifretland.co.uk

Steve Jackson

M: 07789101565
E: stepjack43@hotmail.com
W: stevejacksonillustration.com

Fiona Gowen
20 Middleton Gardens
Gorleston
Great Yarmouth, Norfolk
NR31 7AE

M: 07742791586
E: Fionagowen@gmail.com
W: www.fionagowen.co.uk

Marte Velde Koslung

T: (+47) 98072895 Norway
M: 07985914217
E: marte.velde@gmail.com
W: martevelde.com

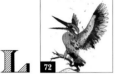

L

72

Jane Laurie
'Homeland'
Salwayash
Bridport, Dorset
DT6 5JE

M: 07870611286
E: crow@janelaurie.com
W: janelaurie.com

M

80

Jenny Marshall

M: 07833116071
E: jennmarshall@hotmail.co.uk
W: jennymarshall.co.uk

74

Nicole Lawson
14 Haw View
Yeadon
Leeds
LS1 97XF

M: 07784627924
E: Scruff_bum@hotmail.com
W: nicolelawson.co.uk

82

Shun Matsuzaka
5-5-9 Oji, Kitaku
Tokyo 114-0002
Japan

T: (+44) 7957195057
E: unko102@hotmail.com
W: illustrashun.com

76

Amy Lewis
3 Church Street
Tywardreath
Par
Cornwall
PL24 2QG

M: 07816260823
E: amy_littleflower@hotmail.com
W: www.mimlewis.co.uk

84

Caroline Metcalfe
22 Woodlands Grove
Stockton Lane
York
Y031 1D

M: 07763059405
E: Cazamataza@hotmail.com
W: www.carolineillustration.co.uk

78

Chloe Luxford
40 Oakdale Road
Liverpool
L22 9QS

M: 07890896050
E: chloeluxford@hotmail.com
W: chloeluxford.co.uk

86

Nick Mott

M: 07821540803
E: nicholasmott@hotmail.co.uk
W: nickmottillustration.com

130

Benjamin Mounsey
19 Penmere Hill
Falmouth
Cornwall
TR11 2RB

M: 07917885753
E: ben.illustration@googlemail.com
W: greenglasses.co.uk

88

David Plant
28 The Dingle
Knighton
Powys
Wales
LD7 1LD

M: 07980089853
E: davidjplant@hotmail.co.uk
W: www.davidjplant.com

96

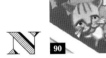

Lauren Nickless
3 River Mead
Ifield Green
Crawley
West Sussex
RH11 0NS

M: 07708935814
E: Loznick@hotmail.co.uk
W: Loznick.com

N 90

Alice Povey
28 Albany Road
Woodhall Spa
Lincolnshire
LN10 6TS

M: 07799338826
E: illustration@alicepovey.co.uk
W: alicepovey.co.uk

98

Lewis Old
5 Greenhill Terrace
St.Martin
Helston, Cornwall
TR126BS

T: +44 (0)1326 231052
M: 07799207111
E: Lewisold@yahoo.com

O 92

Chloe Pyne

M: 07821314809
E: chloe_pyne@hotmail.co.uk
W: chloepyne.co.uk

100

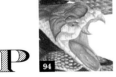

Victoria Parker
6 Aldridge Road,
Ferndown
Dorset
BH22 8LT

M: 07896672088
E: vjparker04@hotmail.com
W: victoriaillustration.co.uk

P 94

Viola Rank-Broadley
Stanfields
Kingscourt Lane
Rodborough, Stroud, Glos
GL5 3QR

T: +44 (0)1453 765985
M: 07811350996
E: viola@violarankbroadley.co.uk
W: www.violarankbroadley.co.uk

R 102

Heather Rothwell

M: 07906586002
E: hello@heatherrothwell.co.uk
W: heatherrothwell.co.uk

104

T

Amy Timms
Rochford House
Church Road
Froxfield
Marlborough
Wiltshire
SN8 3JY

M: 07748876062
E: timmsamy@hotmail.com

112

S

Ellie Kate Sandford
Trelubbas Cottage
Lowertown
Helston
TR13 0BU

M: 07944650010
E: ellie_ctap@yahoo.co.uk
W: elliekateillustration.co.uk

106

Taynee Tinsley
Leicity
13 The Portwey
Leicester
LE5 0PT

T: +44 (0) 1162741880
E: tayneetinsley@hotmail.com
W: taynee.co.uk

114

Kine Jeanette Solberg

T: (+47) 92287539 Norway
M: 07706919637 UK
E: kinesolberg@gmail.com
W: kinesolberg.com

108

W

Solveig Wiig

T: (0047) 412 21 562 Norway
M: (0044) 07985914231 UK
E: solveig.wiig@googlemail.com
W: http://www.bambrez.co.uk/solveig_wiig/index.html
www.solveigwiig.com

116

Fatime Szaszi
5 Harbour Terrace
Falmouth
TR11 2AN

M: 07876045529
E: szaszi.janos@gmail.com
W: fatimeszaszi.com

110

Carys Williams

M: 07969913483
E: pinkertoncarys@hotmail.com
W: caryswilliams.com

118

Angel Toi Hung Wong
Flat C,
5/F Sheeny Terrace
200 Tsuen King Circuit
Tsuen Wan
N.T. Hong Kong

T: +852 24148256 Hong Kong
+44 07796823855 UK
E: toitoi328@gmail.com
W: http://www.toytoi.co.uk

Lisa Zibamanzar-Mofrad
21 Pengarth Rise
Falmouth
Cornwall
TR11 2RR

M: 07877213685
E: lisazillustration@hotmail.co.uk
W: lisazillustration.com

Victoria Wright
8 Glasney Place
Penryn
Cornwall
TR10 8 LN

M: 07866568465
E: vicquigley@hotmail.com
W: www.vwrightillustration.co.uk

UNIVERSITY
COLLEGE FALMOUTH
BA (HONS) ILLUSTRATION

STAFF

Alan Male	Course Leader & Level Three Tutor
Mark Foreman	Level Two Tutor
Nigel Owen	Level One Tutor
Sue Clarke	Senior Lecturer
Mike Venning	Senior Lecturer
Serena Rodgers	Senior Lecturer
Linda Scott	Illustration
Gary Long	Life drawing

Marilyn Towndrow	Visual studies
Rachel Dunn	Visual studies
Mary Mabbutt	Visual studies
Sue Miller	Art direction
Kerryn Roach	Digital imaging & design
Peter Bennett	Graphic design
Stuart Odgers	Printing technology
Karen King	Creative writing

Louise Egger

Sophie Banks

Zoe Bryant

Louise Bartlett

Robert Allwood

Paul Conway

BOOK *of*

QUOTES *and* SAYINGS

2